On the Wings of a Dove

(Grandmother Tales)

N.M. STEPHEN

Illustrated by : Priya Francis

Published by the author 1/26/2009

ISBN: 978-0-6152-8434-7(sc)

*This book is dedicated
to my grandchildren, Benjamin,
Jonathan, Stephen, George, Elizabeth, Sara and Molly*

and

*to the memory of my beloved mother,
Bava, who told me these stories when I was a child*

Table of Contents

WHY THE DOVES CALL KU

Long, long ago, there was a beautiful country called Kanaka Puri, Land of Gold, situated on the slopes between snow-capped mountains in the Himalayas.

True to its name, the country was indeed a paradise on earth. It was filled with stately trees and beautiful flowering plants. Wherever one looked, there were flowers of bright colors and fragrant scents. Springs, streams, and murmuring brooks splashed water happily. Fruit trees, branches laden with juicy fruits, were everywhere.

This was the kingdom of the doves. Only doves could live there. The doves lived happily under a just, kind, and wise dove king and a gracious dove queen. So happy were they that doves chose not to live anywhere else.

In Kanaka Puri lived two dove sisters. The elder was called Kutty and the younger, Kuttathy.

They were the most beautiful doves in the kingdom. Their wings were whiter than snow and their bosoms, soft as silk. They were as pretty as May roses.

Sadly, they lost their parents when Kuttathy was but a little baby. The death of their parents made them very sad. The older sister, Kutty, became both sister and mother to Kuttathy. Kutty did everything she could to make her little sister happy.

They lived in a snug little nest their parents had built for them on the leafy branch of a tall maple tree.

When their parents died, Kuttathy had not even learned to fly. She stayed in their nest, while her sister went out to gather delicious fruits and nuts for food.

When her sister was old enough, Kutty taught her to fly. When she became a good flier, Kuttathy went with her sister wherever she went.

At night Kutty told her sister dove fairy tales. When she fell asleep, she covered Kuttathy with soft, dry moss, and feathers to keep her warm.

They played together, mostly hide and seek in the clouds. In the mornings before the sun rose they'd float in the air side by side, singing dove songs. After dinner, they slept in each other's embrace.

They would collect food and firewood together, and soon Kuttathy was cooking dinner!

Kutty even taught her sister how to build nests and line them with soft feathers. They were very happy.

One day Kutty woke up before daybreak. She woke her sister up and told her, "Today we shall have fried beans for dinner."

"Wow! What a good idea, sister. I love fried beans," Kuttathy said. She remembered the delicious fried bean dinners their parents used to make. Her face brightened at the thought. This was the first time Kutty and Kuttathy were going to fry beans by themselves.

"Then get ready soon. Don't forget your cap and your sun-shades. The sun is too bright and hot for your little, tender head and baby eyes," Kutty said.

"I'll take my little basket too, so that we can collect lots of beans," Kuttathy told her sister.

"Hurry up, darling! We have a long way to go. The bean farm is far off. If we leave now, we can collect enough beans before it becomes too hot."

They flew high, taking care not to drop the baskets held tight in their beaks. They flew over rivers and streams, brooks and meadows. As they flew, they looked down and were thrilled by what they saw below.

"See how beautiful our country is. I am so proud of my country," Kuttathy said.

"So am I," Kutty concurred.

They thought that Kanaka Puri was the most beautiful place in the world.

Kuttathy was proud to be flying with her sister. She loved her sister very much. This was the first time Kutty was taking her sister with her on such a long journey.

She told her sister, "Chechy, elder sister, I am so very lucky. You are the best sister in the world. You love me very much and you take good care of me. Our parents in heaven must be very happy to know that you take such good care of me. I love you, dear sister, more than I love anybody else in the world."

Kutty was pleased, but said, "Do not talk like that, my little darling. I am only doing my duty. Besides, you are a good sister. Nothing I do is too much for you."

Soon, they reached the bean farm. By that time the sun had started to climb up the sky, but it was still not too hot.

By mid-morning, they had collected two baskets full of ripe beans. They flew back, holding the baskets with their beaks.

At home, they emptied the beans into the frying pan. They had collected so much that the beans rose above the pan in a mound.

"You fry the beans while I go and take a bath. Watch the beans carefully and make sure that they don't get burnt," instructed Kutty as she flew away to the little stream near their nest.

At the stream she met friends, who asked her where Kuttathy was because Kutty was rarely seen alone without her sister by her side.

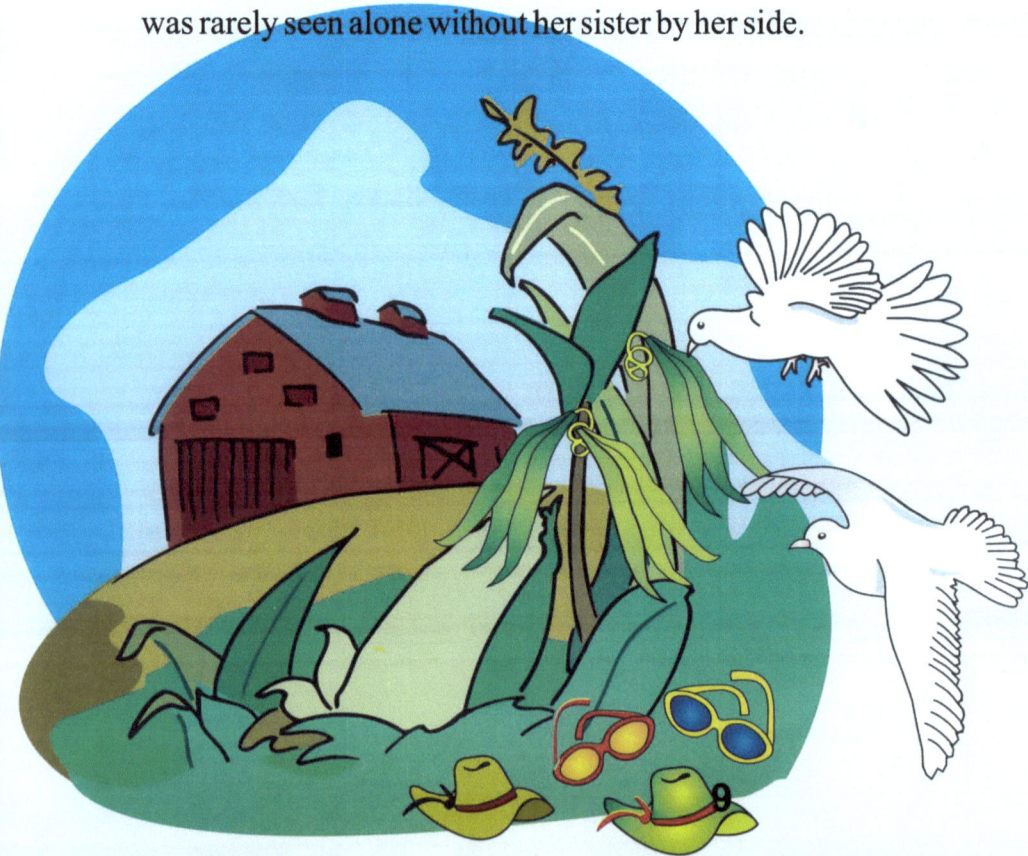

"I have the most loving sister in the world. She is an angel, and I love her very much. She is at home frying the beans we collected this morning," Kutty told her friends. "We are having fried beans for dinner tonight," she added.

Kuttathy lit the fire and started frying the beans. She followed her sister's instructions carefully. She watched the beans constantly and stopped when they turned a golden brown; she was careful not to let them burn.

When she finished frying, she covered the beans with leaves and waited for her sister's return, humming a favorite dove tune.

She was happy because she thought that she had done well and had cooked a great dinner. She was sure her sister would praise her.

She could hardly wait for her sister to return to taste the delicious beans. She could hardly hold herself back from trying some before her sister got back.

When she saw her sister in the distance, she flew out to meet her, and they flew back together.

"See how nice the beans have turned out, how good they smell ! See the golden color," Kuttathy told her sister seated at the dinner table.

Kutty lifted the leaves with her beak and looked inside the frying pan. To Kuttathy's surprise, her sister was mad instead of being pleased. She was very angry and was yelling.

"You, greedy creature! I was a fool to trust you with the beans. The frying pan was filled to the brim with beans when I left, and they rose in a heap above. Now look, how little is left. You ate most of the beans by yourself! Is this how you repay me for all that I have done for you? How could you be so mean?"

"Dear sister, believe me. I did not eat any of the beans. I did not eat even one bean," Kuttathy protested.

But Kutty did not believe her sister.

"I do not trust you anymore," she yelled at her sister. "Go away, and let me not see you again."

Kuttathy pleaded with her sister and tried to convince Kutty of her innocence. But Kutty was not in a mood to listen.

When Kuttathy was convinced that her sister would never believe her, she became very sad. She thought, "My sister is never going to love me again."

She flew around their nest with moist eyes a few times, hoping that her sister would change her mind. Finally, she flew away. She could not bear to live in the dove kingdom anymore and flew far away.

A few days later, Kutty went to collect beans. She was on her own. She put the beans she had collected into the frying pan and fried them.

When they were done, to her surprise, she found that the beans had shriveled while they were cooking, and they seemed much less than when she had started.

The truth dawned in her head. Kuttathy had not eaten any of the beans. She was overcome with grief. She could not eat or sleep. She beat her head against the twigs of the nest.

Hot tears rolled down her cheeks, down the twigs, down branches, down the trunk and dropped on the ground, making the sound of dripping water.

She climbed to the topmost branch of the tree and started calling for her sister.

"Kuttathy, KU-KU-RU-KU-DU! Kuttathy, baby, KU-KU-RU-KU-DU!"

Ever since she has been sitting there, crying and calling for her long lost sister.

Without eating.

Without drinking.

Without sleeping.

"Kuttathy, KU-KU-RU-KU-DU! Kuttathy, baby, KU-KU-RU-KU-DU!"

When the other doves in Kanaka Puri heard the sad story, they joined Kutty in her search for her lost sister Kuttathy, calling:

"Kuttathy, KU-KU-RU-KU-DU! Kuttathy, baby, KU-KU-RU-KU-DU!"

Some doves left Kanaka Puri and traveled to all the corners of the world looking for the long-lost Kuttathy. They still hadn't given up the hope of finding her.

Wherever they went, they called, "Kuttathy, KU-KU-RU-KU-DU! Kuttathy, baby, KU-KU-RU-KU-DU!"

To this day, doves all over the world are still calling for the long-lost sister.

Days come and go.
Months come and go.
Years come and go.
Decades come and go.
Doves have not given up hope of finding her, and they still call, "Kuttathy, KU-KU-RU-KU-DU! Kuttathy, baby, KU-KU-RU-KU-DU!

FIREFLY

In the Beginning, according to one legend, there were no fireflies. God created butterflies, the finest of his creations. It has often been said that God himself was astonished when He saw the exceptional beauty of his own special creation.

The butterflies were very happy. They flitted from one beautiful flower to another, showing off their wings and eating nectar, which they thought, God had created specially for them.

"Finest and sweetest food for God's finest creatures," they thought.

In a far-off land, there lived butterflies that had wings even more colorful than the wings of the butterflies living in all other butterfly colonies. These butterflies became too proud as time passed, and looked down on less beautiful butterflies.

They used to sit on flowers and compare the color of their wings with the color of the flowers on which they sat.

"Are we not more beautiful than these flowers?" they used to ask among themselves. "We are certainly the prettiest things in the world, more beautiful than flowers, the peacock, and even the rainbow."

They became so proud that they started looking down on butterflies that were not as pretty as they were.

"God created us the finest of His creatures. We are far more beautiful than the biggest and the most beautiful flowers. Let the other butterflies collect nectar from the smaller and less beautiful ones," they said.

From then on, they collected nectar only from the finest of flowers and neglected the smaller and less beautiful ones.

The neglected flowers became very sad. They complained to God.

God summoned the proud butterflies before Him. He told them, "You are my finest creation. I gave you colorful wings and the sweetest of foods. Because of these special gifts, you became too proud. "You looked down on creatures that are less fortunate than you. And you ignored some of my other creations. So I am going to take away the wings that made you too proud.

"From now on, instead of colorful wings, you will have hard shells, and you will be called beetles."

So saying, He changed all the proud butterflies into beetles

Amongst the proud butterflies, there were a few that had not liked what their brothers and sisters had been doing.

They had been collecting nectar from the different flowers, big and small, pretty and not so pretty.

These butterflies were very sad. They bent down before God, tears rolling down their cheeks, and begged for mercy.

"Good Lord, have mercy upon us. We did not offend you. We collected nectar from every flower without looking at their beauty, color, or size. Therefore, please do not punish us as you have punished our proud brothers and sisters."

But God was not prepared to forgive them completely. He said, "I know that you did not avoid my less fortunate subjects as the others did. But you knew what they were doing. Why didn't you point out their mistakes and correct them?"

"Since your offence is less serious than that of the others, I'll make your punishment milder.

"You'll be beetles, but with a special gift. You shall have lanterns that will glow in the dark. You'll be called lightning bugs. Some people may even call you glow-worms.

In turn, I expect you to use the light of the lanterns to guide the animals to safety when they get lost in the forest on moonless and starless nights."

That's how fireflies came to be created.

Firefly Song

**Angels received fireflies into the world
with a special firefly song.**

Firefly, firefly, blink and wink.
Firefly, blink,
Firefly, wink.
Firefly, firefly, flicker and flash.
Firefly, flicker,
Firefly, flash.
Firefly, firefly, shimmer and sparkle.
Firefly shimmer,
Firefly sparkle.
Firefly, firefly, light up the path,
With the twinkle of your eyes,
With the lantern in your belly,
With sparks in the dark,
And be the twinkling lights in the night sky.

MANU THE WICKED FISHERMAN

Manu lived with his wife Meena, son Mohan and daughter Manju in a little, old shack by the sea, in India. He was a poor fisherman.

Manu knew a great deal about fishing and fish, and he was able to choose between fish that made good food and those that didn't, fish he could easily sell in the market and those he could not.

But Manu was an unhappy man. He would mumble and grumble and curse his fate. He was easily irritated even by the smallest things and would often yell at his wife and children.

He did not like people who were happy and was jealous of those who were wealthier than him.

Everyday, he went out fishing with his son, while his daughter stayed behind to help her mother with the cooking, and other housework.

He would set out at dawn for the seashore, where he sat all day with the fishing rod in hand and fishing net slung over his shoulder, looking at the fish swimming in the clear water. When he saw the right type of fish, he would cast his net.

If he was lucky, he would catch a lot of fish. Sometimes, he caught nothing and went home empty handed.

Manu was a miser and a vile person. When he earned a lot of money, he never told his wife and children. He hid some of the money. On days he came home empty handed, Manu did not take the money he had hidden to buy food. Instead, he made his wife and children starve.

In another shack, not too far away from them, lived another fisherman, Raja with wife Rema, son Ravi, and daughter Rani.

Although Raja was a poor fisherman like Manu, he was a good man and a very friendly person. He never complained about anything.

He was always happy, and his family, though poor, was always happy too. Manu disliked his neighbor just because he was a happy man and because his family was happy. Whenever he saw Raja, he turned his face away from him.

Manu forbade his wife and children from talking with Raja's family and instructed them to avoid Raja and his family.

Manu felt that God had been unfair to him. He was fed up with the bad food he ate, the poor clothes he wore, and the shack in which he lived.

He did not want to live in his wretched shack any more. He wanted to live in a mansion, eat good food, and wear attractive clothes like the rich people in town.

On the way to the market where he went to sell his catch, he had seen beautiful cottages, with lovely gardens. He had also seen beautiful mansions. He badly wanted to live in a mansion.

In his village, there was a shrine in a thick grove. This was the shrine of Lakshmi, the goddess of wealth. The shrine was hidden from the road.

He thought, "Lakshmi has given wealth to a lot of people. They have great houses and all the good things in the world. The only way to become rich is to please Lakshmi and ask her for a boon."

He made up his mind to do everything to please Lakshmi. He bought jasmine garlands from the market everyday and put them around Lakshmi's neck.

Everyday, he sat before Lakshmi's statue and sang songs of praise. And he lit candles.

He prayed to Lakshmi every morning and every night. He poured out all his problems before her.

Nothing happened for a long time. But he did not give up hope. Instead he spent more time at the shrine and made more offerings.

He kept his visits to the shrine a secret. He did not even tell his wife and children. And friends he had none.

One day, while he was praying, the goddess appeared. Manu prostrated before her.

The goddess told Manu, "You have been praying to me for many years. I am well pleased with you." Then, the goddess asked Manu, "What do you want from me?"

"Great goddess, you know that I am a poor fisherman. I live with my family in a poor shack. We do not have good clothes, and we do not eat good food. Some days we go to bed hungry."

"You have given so much wealth to people who do not deserve all the wealth you have given them. Some of them even do not pray to you. Still you have given them everything they need.

"I have been praying day and night to you and bringing garlands everyday and lighting candles every night. But I still live in poverty."

"I am well pleased with you for being my devotee all these years. I am going to give you a boon," the goddess told Manu.

Manu was happy. He thanked the goddess and waited for the boon. The goddess gave Manu three coconuts.

"Take these coconuts home. They are special coconuts, I brought from heaven. They have the power to make you wealthy and give you whatever you ask for: food, clothes, gold, and mansions. Just take one of these and break it, wishing for whatever you desire to have. They will be delivered to you instantly," said the goddess.

Then she added, "However, there is just one condition. When you get whatever you ask for, your neighbor Raja will get twice as much as you get. If you ask for food, he will get twice as much food. If you ask for wealth, he will get twice as much too. If you ask for one mansion, he will get two."

24

Manu was totally frustrated and unhappy. He thought, "I am the one who has been praying to her. I spent so much money buying garlands and candles for her. It is not fair to reward someone else for what I have done for her. And he is to get twice as much as I!"

He grumbled and muttered and cursed as usual and kept what transpired between him and the goddess a secret. He hid the coconuts in the attic.

In the meantime, life was as miserable, as ever for the family. Then, he did not catch any fish for several days. There was no food in the house and nothing to cook. His wife was very sad. Her children would go hungry. She did not know what to do. Suddenly, she remembered that her husband used to hide money. She searched the whole house: under the beds, inside every basket, in every pot and finally, in the attic.

To her surprise, she saw the coconuts. She thought, "The children can at least eat coconuts tonight."

She took the coconuts to the kitchen and broke one of them. As she was breaking the coconut, she thought, "It would have been great if we had rice and vegetables too. Then I could prepare some dishes to eat with the rice."

She was astonished when she suddenly saw a large basket full of rice and several baskets of different types of vegetables.

She prepared a great feast and waited for her husband's return. When the children saw him at a distance, they ran towards him and told him, "Hurry, a great feast is waiting for you. Mamma prepared so many dishes today."

Manu's face became red with anger. As the children looked at him puzzled, he ran to his neighbor Raja's house, where he found Raja and his family enjoying a great feast. He had even invited some of his neighbors. Raja invited Manu to join them, but he refused and ran away in anger.

Manu was very unhappy. He wanted to punish Raja for enjoying things to which he had no right. He did not eat anything that night and he could not sleep thinking of the injustice.

He spent the night thinking of ways to punish Raja. Finally he had a good idea. Next morning he woke up before his wife and children did. He knew how to punish Raja but did not want his family to know what he planned to do.

He took one of the two remaining coconuts to the backyard and broke it wishing, "Make me blind in one eye."

He lost the sight of his right eye. With the remaining eye, he ran to his neighbor's house. Poor Raja had lost both his eyes. He was very sad. He did not know what he had done to deserve such a severe punishment from God.

The blindness made him invalid. He could not go out of his house without help, and he could no longer go fishing. He did not know what to do.

Raja decided to pray to Lakshmi, the goddess. "Why have you punished me thus? I did not do anything wrong. Even though we are not rich, we have been happy. Now, I don't know how we can make a living. Please, goddess, help us."

Goddess Lakshmi realized what had happened. She called Manu before her and said, "You asked for a boon. I gave you what you asked for. In your jealousy and wickedness you forgot yourself and your family. Instead of enjoying the riches I gave you, you planned evil for your neighbor."

So saying, the goddess took away the remaining coconut from Manu and gave it to Raja with two more, and told him to use them wisely.

After the goddess' departure Raja broke the coconuts wishing for wealth, health and restoration of his eyesight. He got all the wealth he needed and his eye sight was restored.

Raja spent the rest of his life in happiness and Manu remained a poor one-eyed fisherman until his death.

THE VILLAGE SCHOOL TEACHER

Once upon a time, in a faraway land, there was a little village in the foothills of a thickly forested mountain. In the forests lived herds of elephants. So, the village, in the language of the people living there, was called Aanagram. Aana, elephant, and gram, village, so, Elephant Village.

Aanagram was a small village of thatched huts. In those days, there was no electricity or water from taps. People fetched water from wells or mountain streams.

In the middle of the village was the village school. It was just a large, thatched hut. Mr. Hari, the only teacher in the school, lived with his wife and baby girl behind the school in a small hut.

Mr. Hari was a short man with a rather big, round belly. When he moved about among the children in the classroom, his belly jiggled from side to side like the hump of a camel. This made the children laugh.

The children did little tricks to get Mr. Hari excited because when he was excited, he moved faster, and the faster he moved, the faster his belly jiggled. Although he never beat his children, he always had a stick in his hand, which he would shake at them whenever they became too mischievous. That was enough to make them behave.

Mr. Hari was a very kind man and a good teacher, and the people of the village loved him. They all sent their children to his school to be taught not only their reading and writing, and arithmetic, but also to learn their manners, and how to behave properly.

Everyday, children from all over the village came to the school carrying their slates and slate pencils. In those days, children in villages like Aanagram did their work on slates using slate pencils: their parents were too poor to buy paper and pencils for them.

Mr. Hari sometimes used to doze off during classes. When the children heard him snoring, they would stop working and start to move around the classroom and talk.

The naughtier kids played tricks. Little Balu was the naughtiest. He would even dare to creep under Mr. Hari's chair, bare his teeth, and prance like a monkey. This would make the children roar with laughter. Mr. Hari would wake up and angrily shake his stick at the children and that would make the children laugh even more because of how it would make his belly move.

Mr. Hari sneezed often. He would sneeze at the dust from the blackboard, he would sneeze if any of the children had flowers in their hair, which was everyday because in that village people loved flowers. He would sneeze whenever he bent over to check their work on their little slates.

Well-brought-up children everywhere would know to bless the person who sneezes. In Aanagram people said "Shambo, Mahadeva," Praise the Lord, and placed their hands on their chests when someone sneezed. That was how it was done in that land.

Mr. Hari was very particular that his students followed all the village customs very carefully, and it did not matter how many times a day he sneezed, the children all had to stop whatever they were doing and shout "Shambo, Mahadeva," with their hands on their chests. He did not want the villagers to think that he did not teach good manners at his school.

One day Mr. Hari's wife needed water from the nearby well and came over to ask Mr. Hari to fetch it for her. Mr. Hari did not really like to leave his students by themselves, but they all appeared to be hard at work. Moreover, it would take just a minute!

"My wife needs water for cooking lunch, and the well isn't far off, what's the harm," he thought to himself. Off he went, bucket and rope in hand.

As he was drawing water, unfortunately, he slipped and fell into the well.

"Help! Help!" he screamed as he fell. Hearing the sound of a heavy object falling into the water and the cry for help, the children came rushing. They found their teacher spluttering and spattering in the well, barely able to keep his head above water.

When he saw the children above, Mr. Hari shouted, "Quick, grab the rope and throw it down to me."

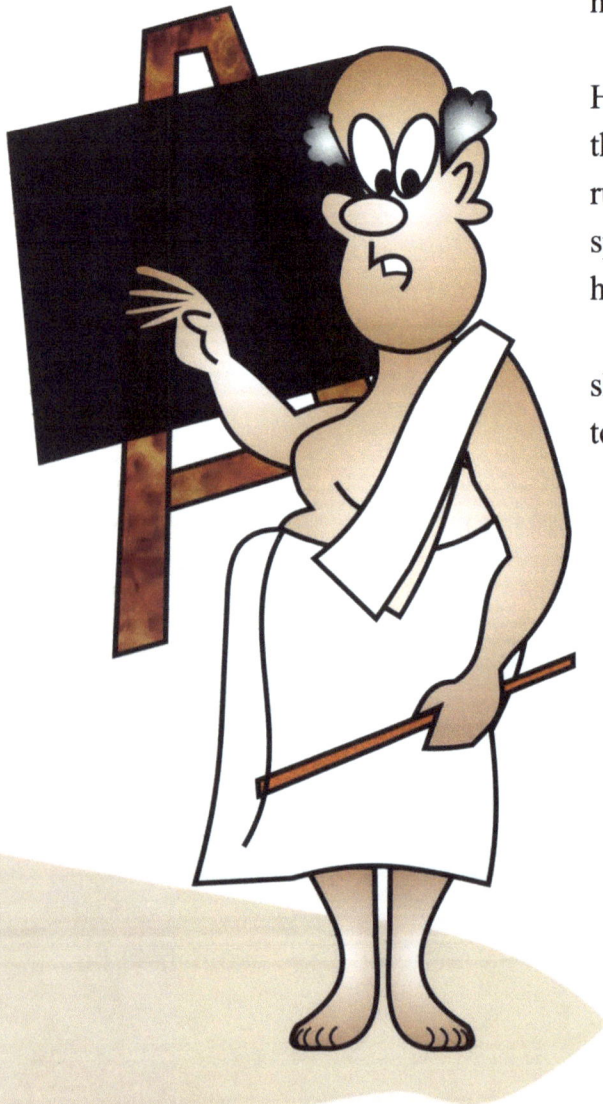

The children did as they were told.

"Now hold that end firmly, as I climb up," he told them.

Mr. Hari caught hold of the end of the rope and slowly and carefully, hand over hand, climbed up.

When he had climbed, but just a little, the cold from his drenched clothes made him shiver and he sneezed loudly.

The sneeze was so loud that it not only deafened the children holding the rope but was heard right across the village.

The children couldn't help themselves: just as they had been so strictly taught they put their hands on their chests and shouted "Shambo, Mahadeva." Naturally, they had to drop the rope to do so.

Down went Mr. Hari into the water with a loud splash. Mr. Hari was getting exhausted, but he told his students, "Let us have another try. Now, hold on to the rope firmly. Do not let it go, whatever happens."

"Yes, Master," they all said, tears running down their cheeks at the sad plight of their beloved teacher.

34

The children held on to the end of the rope, taking their positions, feet dug into the ground to stop being dragged into the well by Mr. Hari's weight. They told Mr. Hari to climb up.

"We will not let go, whatever happens," they said. Reassured, Mr. Hari caught the rope and started to climb. He felt badly like sneezing; remember, Mr. Hari was one who sneezed easily. He tried rubbing his nose against his shoulder and with great difficulty climbed halfway up.

But Mr. Hari could not control himself any longer. With a sound as loud as that of an explosion, he sneezed. The poor children forgot their promises and instantly dropped the rope and crossed their chests and shouted, "Shambo, Mahadeva."

Mr. Hari fell into the water. He drank a lot of water and did not emerge out of water for a long time. The children feared that their dear teacher had drowned. At the top of their voices they shouted for help. The villagers came running.

When he saw Mr. Hari in the water sneezing non-stop and the children shouting "Shambo, Mahadeva," in response, the village chief realized what was happening.

He ordered the villagers to tie one end of the rope to a tree standing nearby and drop the other end down to Mr. Hari. He told Mr. Hari to hold on to the rope and climb up.

Mr. Hari was very tired and extremely cold. But he held on to the rope and climbed. As he climbed, the villagers shouted their encouragement. He climbed slowly and carefully, one hand up at a time. And he sneezed many times and the children said, "Shambo, Mahadeva" each time he sneezed. But the rope held, as it was tied to the tree.

Mr. Hari finally came out of the well safely.

www.ingramcontent.com/pod-product-compliance
Lightning Source LLC
Chambersburg PA
CBHW042114040426
42448CB00003B/271